YOU CAN CARVE

F·A·N·T·A·S·T·I·C

JACK-O-LANTERNS

*The mission of Storey Communications is to serve our customers
by publishing practical information that encourages personal independence
in harmony with the environment.*

Notice

The information in this book is presented in good faith; however, no warranty is given and results cannot be guaranteed. Furthermore, instructions are meant to be safe, and special warnings should be noted. The author and publisher disclaim any liability incurred in connection with the use of this book.

Design by Leslie Morris Noyes
Edited by Kimberly Foster
Production by Carol Jessop and Nancy Lamb
Illustrations by the author
Photos by the author and Lance A. Hart

Printed in the United States by Book Press
Seventh printing, June 1995

CONTENTS

DEDICATION

This book of funny faces is dedicated to my favorite face in the world, my son Lance Jacob Hart.

Each year someone comes up with an even more grotesque, funny, strange, or delightful pumpkin character than the year before. And every year some of us are still staring at the same three triangles and crooked mouth that we managed to etch out once again. No more! Designing and creating a jack-o-lantern is a fun part of a festive occasion and can be a really good chance to express yourself in ways that, at any other time of the year, might be a whole lot less acceptable!

• •

PREPARATION
• •

These are some basic techniques to master. From there the rest is pure play.

Select a pumpkin
Pick one that is evenly shaped and of a size you can deal with. Smaller pumpkins tend to be more limiting, but too large a pumpkin may be more work than you're willing to put in. Occasionally you will find a pumpkin of such an odd shape, or with such a perfectly placed bump, that it suggests its own personality. You can carve some great characters around nature's sense of humor!

Wash your pumpkin
Wash off the pumpkin with a little dish soap and water. Pat dry. Let it dry completely before you transfer the design onto it.

Arrange your work area
Spread out newspapers to hold all that gooey, slimy mess that comes out of the pumpkin. Collect all the utensils you will be using and a picture of what you will carve.

YOU WILL NEED
• •

Design—on paper

Pumpkin— to be transformed!

Tape—to hold design on pumpkin

Nail—to transfer design onto the pumpkin

Potato Peeler—for carving small curves and circles

Paring knife—for carving features. The narrower the blade the better for detail work

Sturdy knife—for cutting out the top of the pumpkin

Sturdy handled spoon—for scraping out the insides of the pumpkin

STEP BY STEP

Take out the top
The first step of actual carving is to cut the top out of the pumpkin. A long knife with a narrow, sharp edge works best. Insert the knife tip pointed at an angle toward the center, and cut around the stem. Remove the blade every few inches, and repeat the process all around the top of the pumpkin.

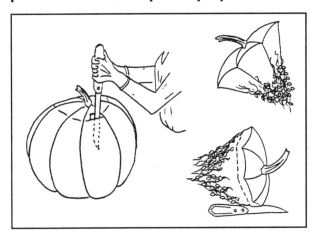

You should have a top piece that is wider at the top than the bottom. This prevents the lid from falling down into the pumpkin after it has dried out and shrunken a bit.

Cut the bottom off the lid.

Remove the insides
Take a sturdy, long-handled spoon and scrape around the inside of the pumpkin to loosen all the strings and seeds. (Don't throw the seeds away—they make a great treat when dried and roasted.) If you are planning to carve a face with a great deal of detail, features will stand out better if you scrape the inside wall of the pumpkin to thin the wall of flesh.

Using a spoon or (Yuk!) your hands, remove all the guck from inside and place it on the newspaper. When you're all done creating, you can just roll up the newspaper and throw it away. Easy clean-up!

PUMPKIN SEEDS
Pumpkin seeds make a delicious snack when dried and toasted. After removing the insides from the pumpkin, separate the seeds from the rest of the mess. Lay them out flat on a cookie sheet, in a single layer, and let them dry for two days in a warm, dry place.

There will be a paper-like film covering them when dry. Rub this off with your fingers. (This really works best outside with a breeze!) Drizzle a little melted butter over the seeds and salt to taste. Roast them in the oven at 350 degrees F. for about 15 minutes. When done they will be light brown. Enjoy!

Transfer design to pumpkin
Now it's time to transfer your design to the pumpkin. If you are a natural artist, you can draw right onto the surface. A grease pencil or a fine-tip felt pen works well. Make sure the pumpkin is dry.

The surest way to transfer a drawing onto a pumpkin is to begin by drawing the character on paper first. Tape the paper onto the pumpkin. You will have to fold little pleats here and there to account for the shape of the pumpkin—just make sure these lie between the features. Using a nail, poke holes through the paper and into the pumpkin, along the lines of the picture. This creates a connect-the-dots pattern on the face of the pumpkin.

Do not let the paper move once you have begun.
This would totally rearrange your design. Take a deep breath and finish what you start with no interruptions.

By taking your smaller knife and connecting the "dots" according to your picture, you will have lines to carve along that look exactly like your planned design, and no unwanted pen or pencil lines.

CARVING

Cut with the knife inserted perpendicular to the wall of the pumpkin, and move the knife away from your body. **Never cut towards yourself** , as you could slip and be hurt.

Never let children work on carving jack-o-lanterns without adult supervision.

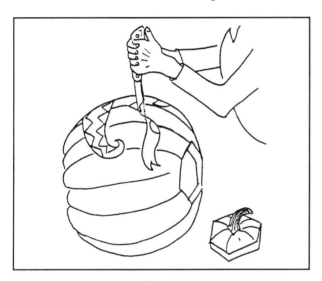

Once a piece is totally cut loose and ready to come off, you can either push it into or out of the pumpkin. Here is a great place to let the kids help. As they push the pieces out of the face, they can see the character take shape.

As you begin to carve the face, you should generally start in the middle of each particular feature and work toward the outside. Take out each feature in small sections (except in cases where the eyes, once removed, are attached to the head as

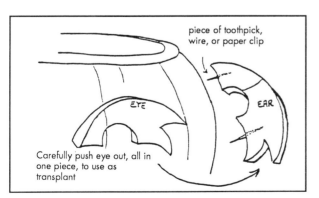

piece of toothpick, wire, or paper clip

EYE

EAR

Carefully push eye out, all in one piece, to use as transplant

ears). It usually works best to do the more de-tailed, or smaller features first. For instance, don't begin by carving a huge mouth, as this weakens the wall of the pumpkin flesh, and it could split as you work on the eyes and nose.

When cutting through to remove a piece, run the knife over the line several times, each time cutting a little deeper. This helps to prevent slipping.

Stop cutting before you reach a corner or end of a line. Remove the knife and insert it into the corner, and with the cutting edge facing the cut you have already made, complete the line. This way you won't cut past the point you intended.

To cut small round holes or detail around fine curves, use a potato peeler.

Shading gives a 3-D appearance. To create the effect, cut along the lines of the feature to a depth of 1/8 to 1/4 inch. Then cut away just the outside flesh between the lines, leaving the lighter-colored inner flesh exposed.

Scoring is carving a shallow line to emphasize a division between features, or to suggest features such as cheeks or worry lines. Follow along the lines with the knife at an angle, and then repeat at an opposing angle to create a "V" shaped trench.

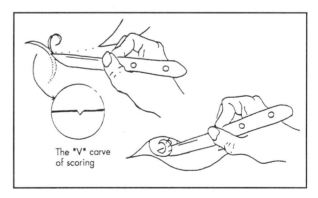

The "V" carve of scoring

Piecing is adding ears or other parts, using parts of the pumpkin or other things, such as gourds . To make ears, cut out the eyes carefully, all in one piece. Then taking a toothpick, a piece of straight-ened paper clip, or any similar surgical implement, push it about halfway into the cutout. Push the cutout into the side of the pumpkin. There you have it, an eye-to-ear transplant!

To add a gourd on as a nose (or ?), cut a hole and insert the "nose" from the inside, pushing it through to the outside.

TRIM

With all the features carved into your jack-o-lantern, you are ready to add the finishing touches. Hold it up to eye level and look into the face. You may see that some of the carving lines don't go straight into the flesh. They may obscure the features once the face is lit from inside, so trim away anything that looks out of place.

PROPS AND SPECIAL EFFECTS

All that's left is to add whatever props you have to your character and you're finished. Be sure any **props are kept away from the candle flame**.

Here are some ideas for creating that **SPECIAL EFFECT...**

Hats, scarves, hair— from a mop top or mohawk, to rope braids.

Ears from posterboard, fabric, gourds.

A little pink (or green, or any color) tongue can be tacked to the inside of the pumpkin and left to hang out of the mouth.

Set the jack-o-lantern up on a pair of **shoes, boots, etc.**

Whiskers—from wire or a broom

Dry ice hidden inside creates an eerie smoky effect.

Paint cheeks, teeth, "eye liner," or the entire pumpkin! How about a black cat, a white skull, a pink elephant, etc.?

Gourds, carrots, parsnips, etc., **for noses, ears.**

Leave your knife with your work—right through the head.

Set three pumpkins up, one on top of the other, snowman style, and carve a face on the topmost.

Or create a whole **"totem pole"** of pumpkin faces. (This is best if held in place by running a rod through the center—an old broom handle will do.)

Bandages, doll arms and legs, a pacifier in the mouth, a mask, craft eyes, fake fur sideburns, or a Cinderella carriage, complete with potato "mice/horses," the rings of Saturn, all the planets, Peter Pumpkin's house...

Let your imagination go!

REPAIRS

Lose a fang? Eyeballs falling out?! Don't panic. One solution is to change your pattern and just say, "I did that on purpose."

Another quick fix is to take a short piece of stiff wire, a piece of straightened paperclip, a toothpick, etc., and push one end into the lost body part, then push the piece back into place. No one will ever know!

DON'T GET BURNED

There are some options to the traditional candle in your jack-o-lantern. Try cutting a hole in the bottom of the backside of the pumpkin and propping a flashlight up through it. Another idea is to cut out the bottom entirely and insert a light fixture or run a strand of Christmas lights through. But for some there is no substitute for the eerie flickering flame of a candle.

If you do use candles, here are some important things to keep in mind.

1. Short, votive candles work best. They can burn down in one night, so you will need a small supply. Before trying to light your candle be sure the wick is free from the wax.

2. Use long, fireplace matches or make a jack-o-lantern lighter. Just by taping a match to a stick or a piece of straightened wire coat hanger, and lighting that with another match, you can save a lot of finger scorching.

3. **Keep LIT jack-o-lanterns away from flammables**—draperies, dried flower arrangements, costumes of children at your doorstep. LOOK and SEE what potential fire danger may be present.

4. **Blow the candle out** before you go to sleep. They do make a dramatic display, but better to let someone miss it than risk a fire.

PATTERNS

PATTERNS

Even though designing your own personal jack-o-lantern is great fun, there are times when it's not always possible. So if you lack the time, or whatever, to sit down and design your very own jack-o-lantern character, here are over thirty patterns to at least get you started. Some of the characters require more attention to detail than others, some are cute, and some are downright evil looking. There is quite a variety, so just pick out your favorite (or favorites) and get started! Happy carving!

Why settle for ...   When just a little more imagination can give you...

Taken just a little further, this can become..."HERE COMES THE SUN"

HERE COMES THE SUN

Carve facial features before ring of flames, beginning with eyebrows. Suggest shading eyebrows and using potato peeler on eyes.

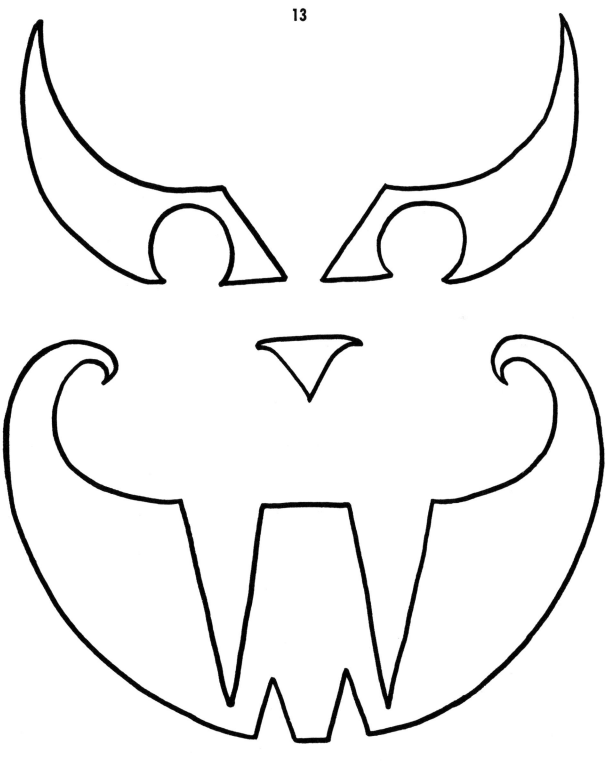

CHESHIRE DEMON

Carve nose and eyes before the mouth. Suggest shading eyes.

GARGOYLE

Shade eyes, but leave outer flesh intact on the small inner triangles.

MASTER EVIL

Shade eyes and/or fangs. Carve mouth last.

BEASTIE

Suggest *either* shading outer portion of eyeball and leaving inner part intact, *or* carving out inner portion (using potato peeler). Also, shade teeth and leave skin on tongue, or vice versa.

GGGGRRROWL!

Shade eyeballs and teeth.

DEMON DOG

Suggest shading outer portion of eyeball and leaving skin on inner triangle.

MANIAC

Shade eyes and teeth, scoring along tongue but leaving the skin on.

WISHY WASHY WORRIER

Shade eyeballs, score worry lines.

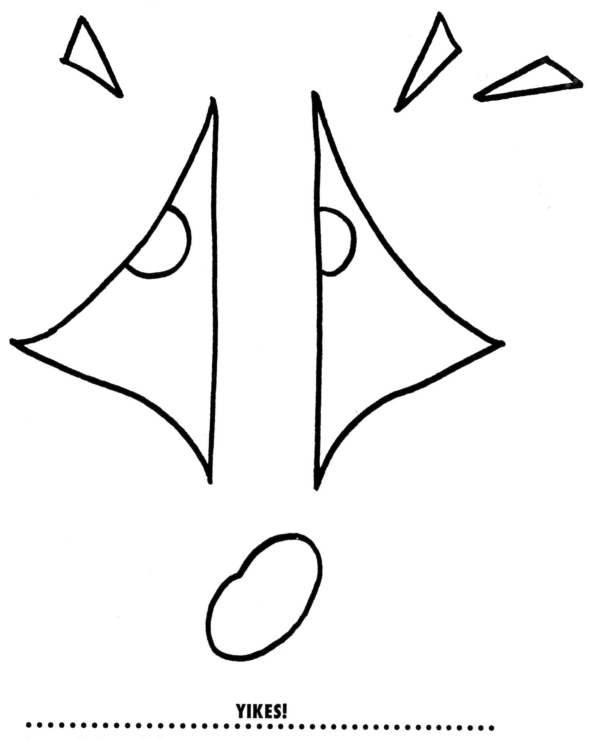

YIKES!

Suggest shading eyeballs.

SLY BY NIGHT

Suggest shading eyes.

CRITTER FACE

Suggest shading eyes and teeth. If eyes are cut out all in one piece, they can be used as ears. Or use bunny ears from posterboard, a raccoon tail wrapped around bottom of pumpkin, or a beaver tail of posterboard.

HOWDY GOOFY

Shade eyes and teeth, leaving skin on tongue.

GRUMBLE FUSS

Shade eyes and exposed fang. Score worry lines but cut clear through for mouth.

SILENT FELINE

Suggest shading eyes except inner triangle.

YEOW!

Shade eyes, except for inner triangle; also shade teeth.

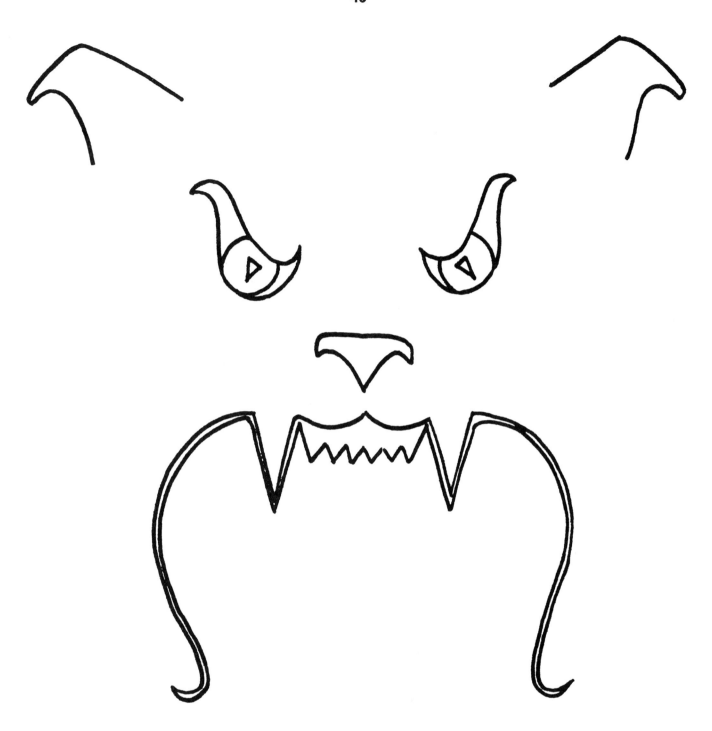

BULLY DOG

. . . .

Shade eyeballs except inner triangle (score around triangle first). Ears can be cut from posterboard and pushed into pumpkin.

OWLY
....
Suggest scoring feathers first, cut through for "wings." When doing eyes start at the inner circle and do outer curves last. Ears can be cut out of posterboard and pushed into pumpkin.

FOWL FACE

Carve inner eyes first and work outwards.

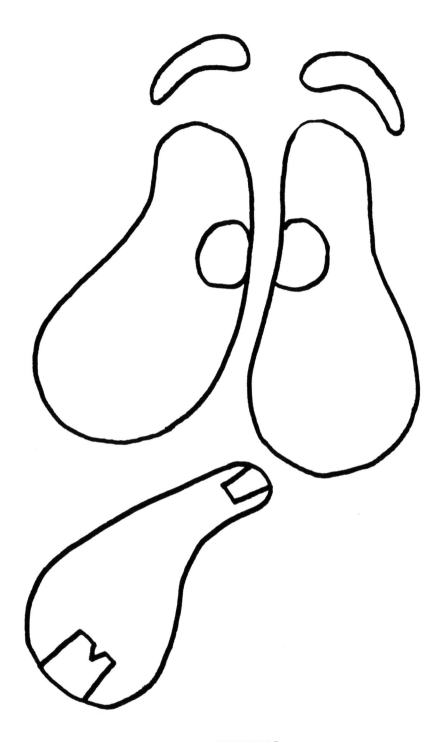

EEEEKS!

Suggest shading eyeballs and teeth.

SKULL

• •

Carve eye area near nose first.

FAT TEDDY BEAR FACE
· ·

Suggest scoring around eyes, shading eyeballs. A small felt tongue can be inserted through mouth line and pinned inside. The eyes can be cut out all in one piece and used as ears.

RACKY RACCOON

• •

Suggest shading eyeballs and teeth.

PIRATE
· ·

Suggest shading tooth. Whiskers are stubs of wire pushing out of pumpkin. Tie a bandana around head and secure with hidden tacks. Cut patch from black felt or fabric. Position over carved scar, wrap ends behind pumpkin, and secure with tacks.

MY LADY

· ·

Shade eyes except inner triangles. Felt pen "eye liner" accentuates eyes. Use a variety of props to suggest different characters, i.e., floozy, witch, nurse, Girl Scout, etc.

DA SHERIFF

• •

Shade inner eye and/or teeth. Carve eyes and buttons with potato peeler.
Moustache of black felt can be glued or pinned on.

LION EYES

Suggest shading fangs. Cut mane and ears to fit from orange posterboard.

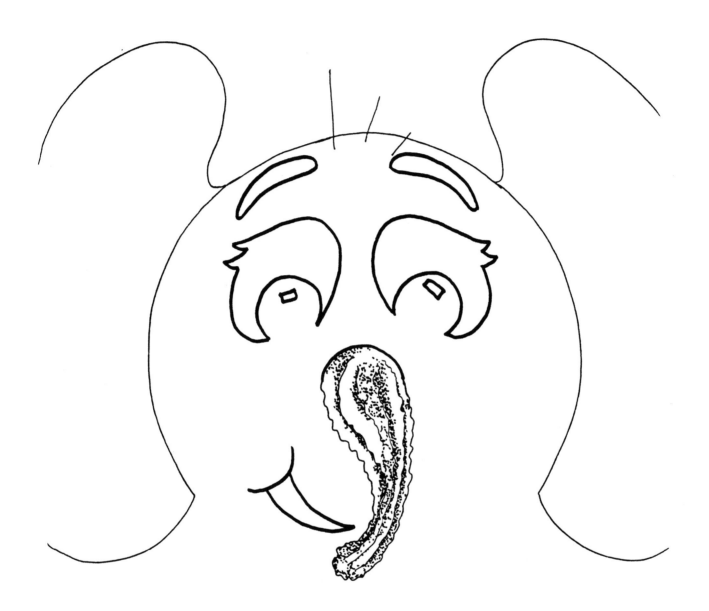

ELTON ELEPHANT

Cut a hole in center of face large enough to push most of a small crook-neck squash through. Cut ears from posterboard, leaving a tab to insert into the pumpkin.

STAR BRIGHT ALL NIGHT

Suggest following pattern all around pumpkin.

HEARTS & FLOWERS

Suggest extending pattern all around pumpkin.

DA SMILEY FACE

Shade teeth and score circle around face.

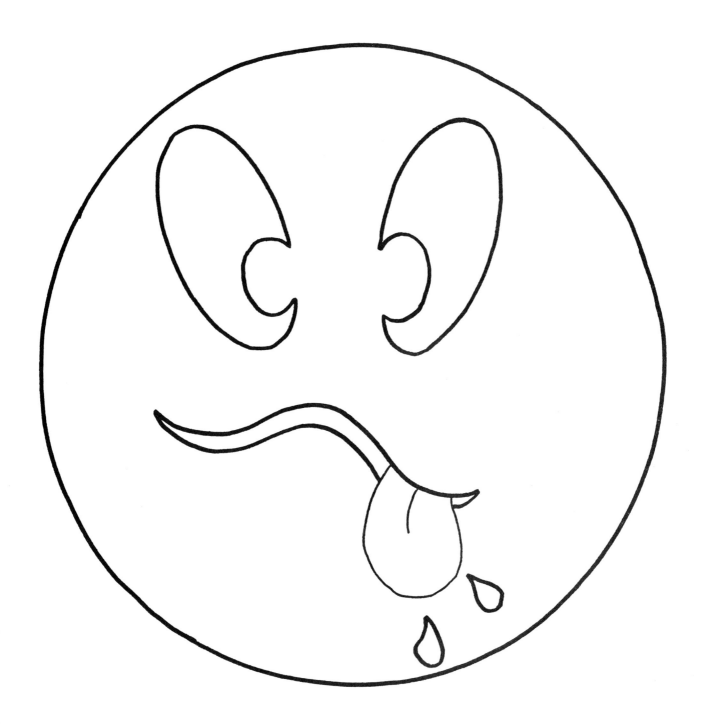

SILLY SLOBBERER

Felt tongue can be pinned inside of pumpkin and pushed out through mouth. Score circle around face.

UCKY YUCKY

Try pinning a green felt tongue to the inside of the pumpkin and pushing it out through the mouth. Score circle around face.

SAY CHEESE

* *

Either cut out every other tooth, *or* shade teeth leaving a thin line of skin in between teeth. Score circle around face.

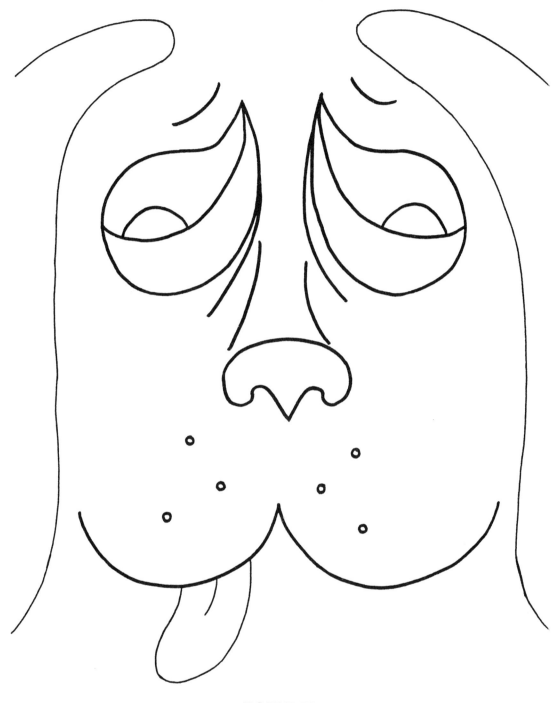

HOUNDED

Cut out felt or fabric ears and tuck under cap. Leave skin on eyeball, shade "bags" under eyes and score wrinkle lines, cut through mouth. Felt tongue can be pinned inside of pumpkin.

LAUGHING PIG

• •

Cut posterboard ears, leaving tab to insert into pumpkin. Eyes can be cut through,
while chins, cheeks, and wrinkles should be scored. Score around nose or fashion a
snout from an empty toilet paper roll and spray it all pink.

LAUGHING CLOWN

Cut through eyes; score wrinkles and cheeks, and around eyes and nose. Paint around eyes with white Halloween makeup, and around nose with red, or paint a 1-1/2" Styrofoam ball red and push part way through cut-out nose hole. Tonsils can be cut from felt and pinned inside.

FRIGHTFUL PUNK'IN

Score worry lines, shade eyes and teeth. Cut out eyes all in one piece and use to make ears. Have fun!

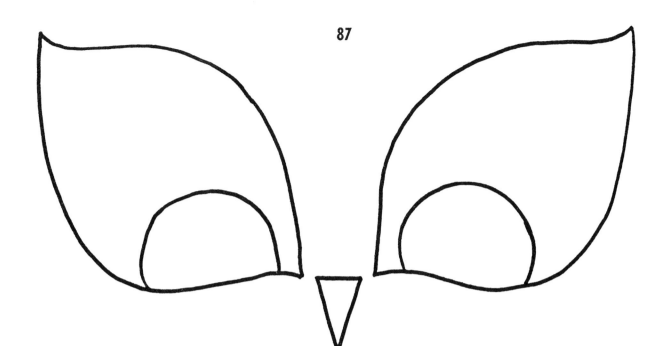

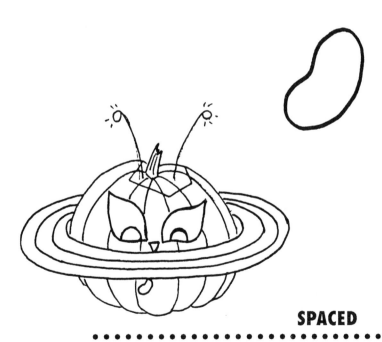

SPACED

Shade eyes. Antennae may be made from 1" Styrofoam balls covered with glue
and rolled in glitter, and 2 pieces of stiff wire (hanger wire). Create rings of
Saturn from posterboard; hold in place with toothpicks.

POLITICAL PUMPKIN

. . . .

Shade eyes. Pin felt tongue inside of pumpkin.

DESIGN YOUR OWN

Designing your jack-o-lantern character can be the most fun of the whole process. Very simple lines can be used to create a range of expressions.

Lines of laughter and happiness turn up, and for sadness, the lines turn down. An expression of fear has wide-opened eyes, while the mouth drops at the corners. In anger the brows come together with an arch and the lip curls. A hearty laugh is illustrated by a wide open mouth and closed or nearly closed eyes. A sneer, worry, a wink, an evil smile, derangement, stupidity, woe—all are suitable expressions for a jack-o-lantern character, but of course the possibilities are limited only by the imagination.

Try mixing and matching the features in the patterns in this book. Make faces in the mirror, check out the comics and the kiddy books, and you'll get lots of interesting ideas.

Enlarging and reducing existing pictures can be done in several ways. Take the picture to a good copy shop—most machines have reducing and enlarging capabilities. Another way is the graph paper method. To do this, trace your picture onto graph paper, or onto paper you have drawn a grid across.

Using either a smaller scale graph paper or grid to reduce, or a larger scale to enlarge, use your original picture as a guide and redraw it onto the new paper. Drawing one square at a time breaks the big picture down into small, simple lines.

Another method is to trace-but-cheat. Trace over your existing picture, but draw just inside the lines to reduce, or just outside the lines to enlarge.

Also, schools and libraries have overhead projectors that take an image from paper and project it onto a screen or the wall. If you have access to one of these, that's another easy way to enlarge a picture.

For further ideas on how to create expressions, look through the following examples for the tell-tale lines. Experiment with different combinations and have fun creating your very own, self-revealing jack-o-lantern!

PAST ITS PRIME

You did it! You created a truly magnificent jack-o-lantern. You got compliments, if not envy, from all who saw it. But now...Halloween is over, and even though a pumpkin is a harvest symbol, don't be tempted to keep your ghoul friend around for Thanksgiving.

Pumpkins rot. They get stinky and slimy, so get rid of it when Halloween is over. People have been known to set them aside and forget about them only to find a pool of caustic slime where they had last seen their precious artwork. The stuff that oozes out of a rotten pumpkin can strip paint, varnish, wax, and who knows what else.

So throw him (or her) away and think of what a great one you'll carve for next year!

ANGER

Arched brows, eyes attached at top, nose placed high, frown with gritted teeth.

DERANGEMENT

Uneven features—"smiling" eye and "evil" eye, exaggerated smile, swirling or panting tongue.

FEAR

Eyes and mouth opened wide, mouth is crooked, teeth show only at edges.

SADNESS

Long drooping eyes, nose placed low, narrow mouth curves down.

WINK

Crow's feet next to closed eye. Smile curves up towards wink.

WORRY

Top of eye deeply arched with eyeball placed at bottom and "focused" on something; worry lines.

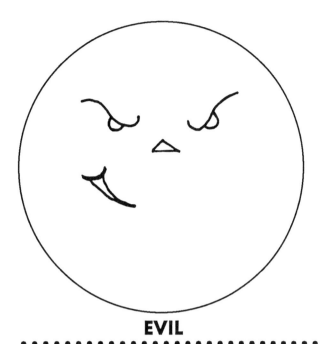

EVIL
· ·
The slight crooked smile suggests a sly secret...

BEFUDDLED
· ·
Eyes focused in different directions. Other features
unbalanced. Tongue hanging.

DOGFACED

· ·

"Animal" nose, large"W"mouth, and loose tongue.

ANIMAL

· ·

Nose in inverted triangle is more animal-like.

HUMAN
Eyes cut out and used as ears. Nose in upright triangle gives human appearance.

FELINE
Almond shaped eyes, "animal" nose, whiskers and "W" mouth.

ANGRY FELINE
Eyes narrow, nose flattens and placed higher on face, lines near eyes and nose for emphasis.

FANGS
Top fangs are usually longer and rest just outside of bottom fangs.